Lucid Dreaming

A Comprehensive Manual For Regulating Dreams To Enhance Sleep Quality, Enhance Creative Thinking, Promote Well-being, And Overcome Nightmares And Sleep Paralysis

(An Introduction To Managing Your Dreams Through Various Methods)

Tomasz Sonnleitner

TABLE OF CONTENT

Overview Of Dream Interpretations 1

Understanding The Science Of Dreams 6

Interpretation Of Dreams 10

How To Prepare For Dreams Of Lucidity 20

Ways To Induce Lucid Dreams 39

Dream Symbols And Indicators: Seeing Patterns In Your Slumber. 59

Gaining Mastery Over Lucid Dream 73

Ways To Interpret Dreams 92

Dream Structure 102

Ways To Get Lucid Dreams 113

In Real Life Versus In Dreams 125

A Guide To Lucid Dream Interpretation 155

Overview Of Dream Interpretations

From the domain of lucid dreams, greetings! Has there ever been a dream where you realized you were dreaming and could actively participate in and direct the events of the dream? This is known as a lucid dream.

Lucid dreaming is the ability to identify that you are dreaming while sleeping. This level of consciousness enables you to actively participate in and control the events that transpire in your dream, enhancing its vividness and lasting impact. When applied as a helpful method, lucid dreaming can assist people in overcoming anxieties and nightmares, developing personally, and resolving issues.

The idea is not new, as evidenced by the numerous references to lucid dreaming in historical novels and folklore. However, it wasn't until the 20th century that scientific research on the topic began. Researchers have found several ways to induce lucid dreaming, which is a verified and real phenomenon.

It is important to remember that each person uniquely experiences lucid dreaming; some people have more control over their dreams than others, and some have more vivid dreams than others. Each person may experience it differently.

So, what exactly is a lucid dream? A person who is experiencing lucid dreaming is aware that they are dreaming. With this understanding, the dreamer gains greater control over the dream by actively participating in and influencing its events.

The ability to overcome fears and nightmares. By acknowledging that you are dreaming, you can take control of your dreams and change their direction. Problem-solving and personal growth can provide an alternative viewpoint on our waking lives.

This chapter will discuss the basics of lucid dreaming, including what it is, how it differs from regular dreaming, and its potential benefits. We will also examine the history of lucid dreaming and the current status of research in this area.

So, if you're ready to learn about the secrets of the mind and lucid dreaming, keep reading! The forthcoming chapters will address the various methods and strategies for inducing lucid dreams, including dream journaling, reality checks, and other approaches, such as overcoming fears and nightmares and using the dream state for reflection and problem-solving.

Don't worry if lucid dreaming is new; mastering it takes time, patience, and practice. It's an adventure. This book aims to provide you with a complete understanding of lucid dreaming and the tools and resources needed to begin exploring the world of lucid dreaming. Let's investigate the fascinating world of lucid dreaming together.

Understanding The Science Of Dreams

Dreams have captivated and confounded people for millennia despite humans having long tried to understand the importance and meaning of dreams. We now know more about the science of dreams and how it relates to lucid dreaming.

Dreams occur when the body is in the Rapid Eye Movement (REM) sleep phase. This stage of sleep, when the brain is at its most active, is also when most of our dreams occur. Throughout the night, several instances of the REM stage last for around 90 minutes.

Several brain regions that are ordinarily inactive when awake become active during the REM phase of sleep due to the brain's intense activity. It is thought that the vivid, often bizarre aspect of dreams comes from this increased activity.

Dreams can be classified into two categories: REM dreams and non-REM dreams. The most vivid and memorable dreams that come to mind when we think of dreams are REM dreams. Conversely, non-REM dreams are less vivid and remembered during non-REM sleep intervals.

Dream content can be very diverse, ranging from commonplace to peculiar. Many factors, such as our thoughts, feelings, and events from the previous day, may influence our dreams. Studies show that dreams often mirror our waking experiences and might provide insight into our inner feelings and thoughts.

Lucid dreaming has been one of the most important subjects of neuroscience investigation. Studies have shown that during lucid dreams, several brain regions, typically inactive, become active during rapid eye movement (REM) sleep. This increased activity is thought to give lucid dreamers increased awareness and control.

In conclusion, understanding the science of dreams is essential to understanding the lucid dreaming phenomenon. Since dreams occur during the rapid eye movement (REM) period of sleep, when the brain is most active, they can be influenced by our feelings, experiences, and thoughts from the previous day. Lucid dreaming is characterized by increased brain activity and consciousness during the REM state and by the ability to actively participate in and guide the events of the dream.

As we go deeper into lucid dreaming, it is imperative to understand the foundations of dream science and how they relate to it. The next chapter will discuss the various approaches and techniques for inducing lucid dreams.

Interpretation Of Dreams

Carl Jung, a well-known expert in dream interpretation, studied under and worked with Sigmund Freud. However, a disagreement on dream theory led to the end of their partnership. The psychologist and psychiatrist Carl Gustav Jung wrote about dreams and their importance. In addition, he was an adept semiotics interpreter and a keen observer of symbolic relationships in psychology.

Jung believed that dreams create a bridge between our conscious and unconscious identities. He claimed that people go through a process in dreams that enables them to adhere to different solutions they get during the day. Even if he disapproved of the need for dream interpretation, his fascination with symbolic meaning has left us abundant literature about semiotics and how they help us understand meaning.

The fundamental source of discord between Jung and Freud was Freud's belief that dreams were an attempt by the subconscious to conceal suffering or the true self from the dreamer's aware consciousness. Jung viewed dreams as a hopeful and revelatory bridge towards self-awareness. This markedly more hopeful interpretation of the importance of dreams threw the entire Freudian interpretative school on its head. When Jung began his research, he added a crucial spiritual component that Freud had not considered.

Jung believed that the only person equipped to interpret dreams was the dreamer. He continued by saying that some symbols belonged to the dreamer specifically and could only be comprehended in particular ways, while others were universal and could be interpreted broadly. Whether dreams were understood or not, Carl Jung maintained that dreams had a unique function in the human mind, serving as a conduit from the subconscious to deliver insight and hidden meaning to the dreamer's waking consciousness.

People need wholeness. Many of us have unseen triggers, suppressed emotions, and life scars that can make that desire seem unreachable and unfulfilled. However, Jung believed that humans may be able to preserve their intellectual and spiritual integrity by employing dreams as a bridge between the aware and subconscious minds. He reasoned that dreams could reduce human suffering by uniting these seemingly diverse worlds—essential components of a bigger whole.

Before Joseph Campbell and possibly having the greatest influence on his writing, Carl Jung's psychology and the fields of spirituality and religion. This course was established when, as a small boy, he said that he felt "nothing" after obtaining his first communion. He wondered how this could occur in the middle of the profound Mass, full of imagery of God's salvific activity via His incarnation in Christ. He asked himself how he could not become spiritually aware after swallowing a bread host, representing the Body of Christ. This got him thinking about how semiotics, or psychological analysis, may be applied to strengthen the intrinsic force of the Mass and the religious community.

Symbols and signs are used in many global religions' liturgical rites, such as the Mass. Jung looked into them and saw psychological realities via their rich symbolic richness that could help people reach the sense of wholeness we all aspire to. Unfortunately, this aspect of his work has been met with a great deal of hostility by religious critics who see him as a challenger to the Church and a pretender to God's kingdom. Jung's sole objective was to find a way to give the Mass and Communion significance to those who, like him as a young kid, had not known the intended enchantment of the Body of Christ. He intended to transform religious symbols into a semiotic space outside the purview of theologians, allowing laypeople to undergo the healing promised by the Church's soteriology or salvation theology.

The relevance of symbols in modern dream interpretation is known to us because of Jung's seminal study of them as portals to meaning that would otherwise remain hidden. His work illuminates the indefinable by creating definitional touchpoints that have a long-lasting effect on dream studies and the pursuit of human completeness through the integration of conscious and subconscious thought processes.

Numerous dream dictionaries are accessible for interpreting the meaning of various objects, animals, and dream sequences. Many of these symbols have universal explanations found in the ancient world and primitive societies. However, the contributions of academics like Sigmund Freud, Carl Jung, and Joseph Campbell have expanded our understanding of many of them. This chapter aims to help you understand how to interpret your dreams.

Do your dreams have deeper meanings?

It is stated that dreams with the greatest significance occur between 2:00 and 7:00 in the morning. This makes sense, considering how the brain processes information during the sleep cycle. Meanwhile, all of this is based on the assumption that you regularly go to bed by 9:00 or 11:00 p.m. Not only can sleep duration and regularity impact the amount of sleep you get, but they can also impact the quality of your dreams.

Have you ever had a dream in which you fell from a cliff? Simultaneously, you may have been the one to roll off the bed, or you may have been the one to roll off. In your dream, your subconscious tells you to acknowledge that you are getting out of bed. It's also possible that you are in stage I of sleep, which is distinguished by the feeling that you are about to fall asleep. The medical term for this phenomenon, hypnicmyoclonia, is derived from the Greek words for "sleep" and "muscle twitch," indicating how common it is. This event, commonly characterized by a hypnic jerk called a sleep start, may also be accompanied by fast breathing and heart rate. Individuals who have gone through it have likened it to plunging over a precipice.

Dreams about your physical environment have little or nothing to do with significance. For instance, it wouldn't greatly impact your life if you dreamed that something noisy was made. Sometimes, your subconscious mind will incorporate your physical environment and what is happening in it into your dreams. In a dream, for instance, you might be attempting to buzz in to respond to a game show. Perhaps, after all, the baby monitor was humming. Alternatively, it could be because the noise is getting lighter in your subconscious state, and you are getting closer to being awake at this time in your sleep cycle. In either case, it could be an attempt by your mind to rouse you up.

Another alternative is that, despite the likelihood that your dream is important, it could just be the result of external stimuli disturbing your sleep, which your body interprets as a dream. As was previously indicated, your body is indeed sleeping, but your brain perceives the external stimulus from the baby monitor as a dream. We call this procedure dream integration.

Certain elements are often present in the dreams of many people. These dreams can arouse a wide range of emotions. These dreams make sense easily.

How To Prepare For Dreams Of Lucidity

Gaining and maintaining transparency in your dreams requires preparation and a commitment to consistent practice. This chapter covers preparation for your lucid dreaming journey, including maintaining a dream journal, following a sleep schedule, and using tools and resources to enhance your dream experience.

Dream Journal: Keeping a dream journal helps you become more aware of your dreams and helps you recognize patterns and themes in your dream world, which is a helpful technique for preparing for lucid dreaming. Dream journaling, which you can do as soon as you wake up each morning, can help you remember your dreams better and preserve a record of your experiences for later use.

In your dream journal, you should include as much as possible, including the time you went to bed, any events or activities you engaged in before drifting off to sleep, and the emotions and sensations you encountered during the dream. With this knowledge, you can look for trends and cues in your dreams that could help you achieve clarity.

Essential to increasing your chances of achieving and maintaining dream clarity. This means establishing a regular wake-up and bedtime each day, even on the weekends. Regular sleep patterns not only assist the body in maintaining its natural sleep-wake cycle but also increase the likelihood of having lucid dreams.

Tools and Aids: Besides maintaining a dream journal and following a regular sleep schedule, enhance your dream experience and increase the likelihood of achieving clarity.

Lucid dream inducers: The two primary stimulants employed by lucid dream induction devices, such as masks and headphones, are light and music. The signals the devices produce during the REM stage of sleep—such as flashing lights or sounds—can help induce lucid dreams.

Added Resources for Lucid Dreams: Plants and nutrients such as choline, B6, and galantamine are believed to increase the likelihood of having lucid dreams. A neurotransmitter associated with more vivid dreams and the ability to dream coherently.

To sum up, creating a dream journal, maintaining a sleep schedule, and using resources and support to enhance your dream experience are all essential aspects of being ready for lucid dreaming. By following these instructions, you can experience the remarkable potential and power of lucid dreaming.

Reality testing and affirmations in creating and maintaining dream lucidity.

Chapter 10: Combining Inductive Techniques

Well done for making it this far in your lucid dreaming journey! At this point, you are aware of the various kinds of induction techniques and their applications. As you continue to find your special route to lucid dreaming, you may ask how to develop your practice. Concept of combining induction techniques to offer a more successful and personalized lucid dreaming technique.

This chapter aims to provide you with a more in-depth and focused look at combining induction tactics. While we have touched on this topic in passing in previous chapters, in this chapter, we will go into greater detail and offer strategies, advice, and examples for effectively combining techniques.

Benefits that could arise from taking this action.

Maximizing your lucid dreaming practice by using multiple induction strategies simultaneously. With this understanding, you'll be able to successfully experience and manage your dreams and more effectively customize your lucid dreaming experience. Let's now investigate the fascinating topic of mixing induction techniques to maximize your experience with lucid dreaming!

Blending of Methods

Understanding how different induction techniques interact with one another is essential to maximizing the effectiveness of your combined approach. When you begin experimenting with various strategies, you may discover that some complement one another exceptionally well, while others may have diminishing effects or operate against one another. Finding and utilizing these synergies is the key to successfully integrating induction techniques.

For instance, you may discover that the enhanced awareness and better dream recall from the WBTB approach increase the power of your MILD affirmations when combined with WBTB. This combination might have a strong synergistic effect that increases your likelihood of becoming lucid.

Likewise, including DILD in reality checks and dream journaling will improve your ability to recognize dream symbols and trigger lucidity. Combining the two techniques effectively teaches your brain to become more attuned to the dream state and prepared for lucidity.

On the other hand, attempting to combine techniques that might disagree with one another would not be advantageous. For example, it could be challenging to combine SSILD and WILD simultaneously because SSILD fosters a more subdued and passive awareness, whereas WILD demands a sharp focus.

In these situations, it is critical to recognize potential issues and adjust your approach accordingly.

For you to fully comprehend the interplay of these tactics, let me share a bit about myself. I had trouble continuously applying the MILD approach when I initially started lucid dream exploration. However, I noticed a significant improvement in my ability to become lucid once I started utilizing reality checks and WBTB in my practice. Combining these techniques produced a synergistic effect that was more than the sum of its parts, allowing me to enjoy more frequent and vivid lucid dreams.

This experiment taught me how crucial it is to recognize and utilize the synergies across induction tactics. You can modify your approach to better suit your needs and tastes by being aware of each technique's unique benefits and drawbacks and how they complement one another. Ultimately, this personalized method will enhance your lucid dreaming skills and assist you in realizing your full potential in the dream world.

Martina and I were at Atlantic.

Is anyone still here? You must be waiting to hear about the common denominator, that icky glue that seeps into the atmosphere of our world, am I right? I would advise against thinking about or attempting to solve it, for heaven's sake. Not because you can't, but because the correct answer is nonsensical, you won't. Remember that wise realization that you can never find the right answer to a badly posed question? To find the answer here, you must discard everything that provided meaning to your existence. Are you curious about the path you plan to take? An elusive chance to get something that will not help you in your day-to-day life. Do you not find this to be absurd? Before your naive neighbour obtained a car loan and bought a neglected piece of junk, which he now rides around haughtily as if he were the ruler of life itself, this rubbish would have made you look silly.

That has to be a natural talent of mine, and it has to be why I fell in love with Martina. She always made me think twice about things I had taken for granted, and you are wrong if you think you can get used to it. That was her essence. That being said, there's no denying that the first encounter is the most memorable after travelling three thousand miles by bus and plane. Here, I would spend the next two years as a seventeen-year-old virgin who loved women and wished she could spend more time with one of their gorgeous numbers. I mustered the bravery to call out my name from the top of the bus (as needed), even though I was overcome by the urgent need to speak in English. In the following moment, I was engulfed in a tsunami of sound as the assembled group roared and pounded spoons against pots (also traditionally). I was unaware that this was just the start of the homage.

I was pretty busy, so I'm unsure what other individuals were thinking. After completing my scan of the crowd, I melted into it, observing all the lovely girls, of which there were plenty. I was thinking about the three other boys I would have to share a room with and my new roommate, a thoughtful second-year who had come to pick me up. In the steaming Welsh evening air, he reminded me that my bags were still in the belly of the bus, something I had completely forgotten about. With extraordinary agility for his age, the driver was already diving for the suitcases, maybe in an attempt to escape the raucous sounds.

Even if he hadn't quite reached mine yet, relieved that it had not been lost over the long voyage, I took another deep breath and turned back to the door, only to practically freeze, fall deaf and dumb, and liquify into something immensely, irrevocably, simply sublime.

The instant I spotted her before she yelled her name was like a strike to the solar plexus. I heard her voice like someone slicing my throat with a blade. And when I found out a moment later that her name was Martina, I could only compare it to being shot in the heart.

There was another explosion of saucepans, and my roommate asked gently whether any of the bags that had been removed belonged to me, but he seemed to be asking a dead person a question. She was kissing a brassy bad girl who reminded me a lot of my roommate and would joyfully grab her as soon as her shoes reached the floor, and I felt like I was in another universe. Because of the shoes' colour, there is nothing about the owner's look. Never before had I laid eyes on a more ideal hue of blue—let alone on someone's feet. But I had no time to think about it because my angel was approaching me with her flashy companion. Her light grey slacks flowed elegantly over the somewhat overgrown emerald grass, her heels gleaming brightly against it.

I forced a nice smile on my face despite my stumbles. To my surprise, she passed me by as if I were a concrete column, giving me no recognition for this accomplishment. I looked back at her in disbelief as she waited for her two orange suitcases to be placed before her. I thought those men's orange tags looked quite pretty, with just the word "Heavy" printed on them. The edge of her burgundy sweater nearly touched mine on her beautiful shoulder. I was almost done formulating an offer to help take those bags to her house, wherever it was (damn it!). However, the brave girl introduced me to two bold, gorgeous boys who were physically stronger than me. Before taking off, she gestured to the baggage and swiped an authoritative finger with an elaborately painted nail. Just enough, but just enough, for me to sneeze was caused by a gust of wind that raised a tendril of Martina's hair and, as if to taunt me, brushed it beneath my nose like a match against the box. Martina trailed after, her perfume wafting behind her.

A sneeze woke me up; I was lost in a strange country and didn't know what to do. I prepared for anything by packing my bag. I gave up on the idea that we would live together since, regrettably, the roommate led me on a different road than the one selected by my love (yes, it was love, and it was love at first sight, too). Something went wrong, biting into my consciousness, which was already battered from not being able to process most of the words that were coming at me from all sides. In such a small school, I tried to tell myself this was acceptable, even helpful. I was told proudly when I arrived that my new home, a dilapidated two-story building named Sunley, was the newest on campus. I had been riding the bus with Molly for three and a half hours without realizing she was there.

Ways To Induce Lucid Dreams

Exceptional experiences can arise from using lucid dreaming to explore your psyche. Just as everyone responds to situations differently, there are a variety of techniques to employ when attempting to generate a lucid dream.

If you put forth a little effort, you can have vivid, realistic dreams!

Examine the following induction methods, which are not presented in any particular order. While they all differ differently, they also share certain characteristics.

Remember that this is all about YOU at all times. It doesn't matter what other people think is the best method. As this is your experience, behave in a way that benefits YOU the most.

Awakened (Reckless) Lucid Dreaming

When you enter a dream straight out of your awake state, it's known as a wake-initiated lucid dream, or WILD. For this, binaural beats in music or guided hypnosis are frequently utilized.

Binaural beat treatment is a more recent form of sound wave therapy. It uses the fact that the right and left ears are getting the same tone, even if the brain perceives them to be receiving slightly different frequency tones. The binaural beats' modification of brain wave frequency. Binaural beats on the gamma frequency are the best music to listen to when experiencing lucid dreams since this frequency stimulates the gamma brain.

The best mood for this is one of total relaxation and ease. Do an eye mask and headphones, then permit yourself to fully immerse yourself in the present.

You have the freedom to choose the music you like. If you are new to this, beginning with a guided meditation is helpful. By doing this while you listen, you may be able to train your mind to stay alert while your body sleeps.

In essence, you may train it to become your avatar by learning to completely relax your body. When the avatar nods off, your party can begin.

While WILD is simple to learn, it's not that easy.

Your chances of experiencing WILD will increase if you use the other techniques for lucid dream induction.

Verifying the Real World

This method involves asking yourself whether you dream frequently during the day, hoping it may eventually find its way into your actual dreams.

Reality testing, sometimes known as reality checking, is one mental training method. It improves metacognition by teaching your mind to become aware of your consciousness.

In general, whether awake or asleep, you possess the same amount of "awareness".

The idea behind this is that your brain will become accustomed to performing reality checks when you're asleep if you practice them often when you're awake. Stated differently, your training will help your dream.

How does one approach such a task?

Just be sure that the results are different in dream and wake states, regardless of your chosen reality check method. Regularly reviewing your waking world is priming yourself for greater self-awareness in dreams.

Two essential elements are involved in performing a reality check:

Ever ask yourself, "Am I dreaming?"

Look at you. What grabs your interest?

Typical things you might focus on include the following:

Mirrors: Check to make sure your reflection seems normal.

Solid objects: Could you squeeze a hand through a wall or your other hand?

Do your hands look normal, or as if they were from a Ripley's Believe It or Not?

Moment: The hands on a clock will constantly be moving in your dream. However, if you're awake, the time won't truly change.

Inhaling: Pinch your nose and see what occurs. If you're still breathing, you're dreaming.

It is suggested that you select one reality check and carry it out multiple times every day. Training your mind to repeat the reality checks while you're dreaming can result in lucid dreams. That is our desired outcome.

Section Two: TWO WAYS TO GENERATE LUCID DREAMS

1. Dream-induced lucid dreams, or DILDs, start ordinarily before suddenly becoming focused when the dreamer realizes it's a dream.

2. Wake-induced Lucid Dreams (WILDs): dreams that arise from an awake, meditative state in which the waking and dream domains are not consciously separated.

To become lucid in that way, you must recognize that you are dreaming at that moment. Let's focus on the first way (DILD), as it is much easier for beginners. Raising your self-awareness while awake and on the verge of sleep and wakefulness.

- meditation
- Self-hypnosis
- Visualizations
- Reality checks,
- Dream medicines.

Many people can have their first lucid dream within a few days or weeks using some or all of these strategies. Whether you utilize WILDs or DILDs, clarity can be induced more easily with practice.

What Benefits Are Provided by Lucid Dreaming?

First and foremost, Many prefer to use it because it offers them a means of escape. You can fly over breathtaking scenery, see your favourite celebrity in person, teleport to the edge of the universe, or transform into a ninja assassin in a virtual reality fantasy setting. It's much more realistic than daydreaming or playing your favourite video game. Guided dreams are exceptionally vivid.

Aside from arousing interest, conscious dreaming has several benefits, including:

- Finding inspiration to create original music and art; • Solving emotional, mental, and technical issues

- Gaining proficiency in new skills, like martial arts or guitar playing; • Getting over anxieties, such as public speaking or phobias; • Communicating with your subconscious

Lucid dreams offer an effective psychological means of exploring one's inner self. Whether you are a rookie, moderate, or experienced lucid dreamer, you are in for an unending personal adventure.

Why Start Having Lucid Dreams?

In the past three years, the number of people searching for "lucid dreaming" on Google has increased by almost 300%, and the figure is continuing to grow every month, indicating a significant increase in interest in lucid dreaming. Thanks to movies like Inception, people are beginning to understand that getting eight hours of sleep every night may do more for you than just letting you lie there unconscious.

Nevertheless, despite this massive surge in interest, only a small fraction of these individuals become frequent and excellent lucid dreamers. This is because, despite encouraging developments in the strategies and resources available to help people learn, learning is still far from a precise science. This means that it takes effort, time, and patience.

So, the key question is: Is it worth it? Is it worth devoting time to mastering the art of achieving surreal experiences?

How long does the process take?

Because dreams come from your subconscious, various factors based on your particular psychological composition can affect how easily you can attain lucid dreaming.

Dr Stephen La Berge, one of the pioneers of modern lucid dreaming, taught himself to have lucid dreams "on demand" over three years. However, because the discipline was still in its infancy when he began, he had to start many of the procedures from scratch. Fortunately, many resources and active online forums are available for information.

Most people can have their first lucid dream three to twenty days after they start practising. It will probably take a year or more to dream every night. To do this, you must establish specific routines and perform the fundamental workouts nearly daily.

Techniques for escaping the body

Methods of Projecting Astral Images

Numerous societies have found ways to go into the astral plane. This is great for those who would rather experiment with different approaches to see what works best for us.

Although it's not impossible, most people don't naturally excel at it or come effortlessly to astral projection. Many of us find it difficult to change our thinking since we grew up in a culture that disbelieves in spiritual reality and only accepts reality as determined by science and factual evidence. These self-limiting beliefs might impede our attempts to enter the heavenly realms, and it can be challenging to overcome our cultural conditioning. It takes practice to get past these mental obstacles. You will succeed if you keep your mind on things and apply your chosen strategies with diligence.

Blue Wave Approach

The blue wave method is perhaps the most popular and effective method of producing astral projection. Starting an astral projection experience with guided meditation has the primary benefit of allowing you to actively choose to have an experience in which you have total control.

The disadvantage of the Blue Wave method is that it makes it harder to truly go into a trance state while under control. This is because it is more difficult to overcome fear and conditioning. For individuals who want to take things more slowly, practising astral projection through guided meditation might be quite beneficial rather than diving straight into it in other ways. Understanding your limitations and skills is essential when choosing your astral projection technique.

Making Use of Your Noses

The ear-nose method is most likely the most often utilized. Robert Bruce is credited with creating the Ear Nose Technique.

Start by inducing a trance through deep breathing and meditation. The objective is to reduce stress as much as possible without falling asleep. Certain forms of the technique instruct you to look intently at a tangible object in the room until you can see it well enough in your mind's eye to avoid dozing off. When you're ready for even more relaxation, close your eyes and recall the picture of the thing. Thanks to this, your mind will remain alert as your body drifts to sleep.

You will eventually begin to feel a strange vibration all over your body. Your physical body is just now giving way to your energetic one. Give in and enjoy the rush.

Before trying to escape your body, you must understand how to control the vibrations. If you don't have this level of control, you won't be able to direct the rest of your experience. Use your awareness of the waves in your body to control their onset, frequency, and cessation. Once you acquire this level of total control over the vibrations, you are ready to move on to the next phase of the technique.

Next, picture a long rope dangling from the ceiling above your body. Imagine your spiritual hands rising from your physical hands to grab this rope. "Feel" the line in your hands, the width, the texture, etc. Stop and reintegrate your hand into your body when your vision is as firm as you want it to be. Get back into a focused, mindful mindset.

Taking a break between your first partial and full separation will also help to keep you in control of your experience. Once you're ready, follow the previous steps up to the point when you grab the rope.

But you're going to persevere this time. Gradually, I begin drawing down on the line. By doing this, you will be severing your spiritual body from your bodily body. As you continue, the vibration will become more intense and frequent. You may even feel a paralyzing sensation throughout your body while doing this. When your voyage out of your physical body is complete, you will be in your astral body.

On your first try, don't go outside your house. Explore your room in your astral body, go through the walls, and find other parts of your house.

Technique of Disengagement

Renowned astral travel expert Robert Monroe created this technique.

The Detachment Technique cannot be practised until you have reached a hypnagogic phase. We are not awake at this level of consciousness, yet we are somewhat alert. To reach this peaceful condition without falling asleep, you must first engage in deep relaxation and meditation.

Deepen your trance by relaxing even more after you've attained the hypnagogic state, which is a state of complete relaxation. Keep your gaze fixed on the blackness just outside your eyelids to stay alert. Next, the Rope Technique specifies that a vibrating condition must be induced. As soon as the vibrations begin, behave similarly, allowing yourself to become accustomed to them before learning how to control them. Flip yourself over mentally and land on your bed when the waves get bigger, and your energetic body is ready to leave your body. After that, you are free to relocate as you like.

Dream Symbols And Indicators: Seeing Patterns In Your Slumber.

Have you ever wondered why you experience flying or falling nightmares so often? Or why do particular people or places keep appearing in your dreams? Dreams are replete with hints and symbolism, each with a unique lesson. If you have ever been puzzled by these mysteries of the night, you are about to embark on a fascinating journey. By the end of this chapter, you will possess the knowledge and abilities needed to interpret and understand the clues and symbols in your dreams. But first, what makes this decoding artwork so significant?

Interpreting dream symbols is like learning a new language. Mind, the places that contain your most valuable intuitions, your biggest fears, and your greatest desires. It also gives you a new way to communicate with your subconscious. As you explore this dreamscape, picture yourself being able to comprehend and make full use of these nocturnal visions with the help of a guide. Yes, it would be good.

You most definitely do, and you're not alone in your feelings. Carl Jung explored in "Man and His Symbols" (1964) the notion that dreams are a universal language, full of symbols that, while personal, have common resonances among people, regardless of their cultural background. Jung believed these symbols were key to understanding our place in the cosmos and solving our innermost issues. If I told you that you could understand this language and these symbols and, in the process, discover yourself in a way you never imagined, how would you feel?

One thing you should remember before delving deeply into this symbolic cosmos is that, despite popular interpretations, the most authentic and significant relationship you may have with your dreams is unique. It is true that some reference works, like the well-known "Dictionary of Symbols" by J.E. Cirlot (1962), offer comprehensive explanations. Even with the assistance of these advisors, you should always follow your gut and inner guidance. After all, who is more qualified than you to interpret the signals your mind is trying to send?

In addition to teaching you how to interpret the most common symbols in dreams. It's important to take your time here. Dream interpretation is both an art and a science. Above all, it's important to reflect on yourself, practice, and persevere.

Famous author Herman Hesse said, "The bird struggles to get out of the egg," in "Demian" (1919). The egg is the planet. Whoever desires to be born must demolish a world." The "world" in this context relates to how we superficially understand dreams and symbols. Breaking that egg entails a meaningful journey to learn more about oneself.

Dear reader, are you ready to split open your egg and reveal the delicacies inside? If so, give a deep exhale and continue. Because the dream world is waiting for you, brimming with symbols and hints that only a bold and curious dreamer like yourself could decipher.

Symbols are points of reference in the vast tapestry of our dreams that aid in our understanding of the outside world and ourselves. Each person has a unique relationship with their dream symbols, some common ones being demystified and studied by experts worldwide.

Think about what it would be like to fly in a dream. In "The Interpreter of Dreams" (1899), Sigmund Freud conjectures that the ability to fly might represent the desire to break free from the constraints and limitations of everyday existence. While soaring over cities and scenery, perhaps you're seeking a respite from anything in your daily life. Or are you considering a desire for adaptability and development? Conversely, Carl Jung would argue that flight is a sign of heightened awareness or enlightenment. Isn't it remarkable how unique and important even the most straightforward dream act may be? Or consider the common urge to pursue one's goals. Knowing that your attacker is never far away and is never fully visible could make you run in a panic. Julia Kristeva discusses this type of dream in "Powers of Perversion" (1982) as a metaphor for facing oneself, or more accurately, a rejected aspect of oneself. It could be any feeling you have avoided experiencing in the real world, like regret or dread.

You're probably thinking, "This sounds fascinating, but how do I know which interpretation is right for me?" at this point. Though it may appear mysterious, the answer is both, and neither could be. Dream interpretation is lovely since it is subjective. While many theories—including those of Freud, Jung, Kristeva, and others—provide useful frameworks, the real meaning of dream symbolism ultimately comes from your interpretation and what resonates with you.

One could easily become overwhelmed by the sheer quantity of possible interpretations. However, as we covered in Chapter 8, dream journals can help with that. You will begin to identify recurring themes and symbols if you journal your dreams and review them frequently. And soon, the meanings behind those symbols—those specific to you—will begin to emerge.

Remember how we said that deciphering dreams is like learning a new language? Think of these concepts as a dictionary of grammar and vocabulary. They provide you with the basics, but practice and immersion are the only ways to become proficient.

So I beg you, please, to get going. To look into, question, and face. Additionally, as you move on, remember Anais Nin's assertion that "we dream of giving meaning to everything that would otherwise be meaningless".

Let's examine some more actual cases in detail after reviewing the basic theories and concepts about symbols in dreams. By reading these stories, we may begin to tie up the loose ends and apply what we have learned to real-world situations.

Waking-Induced Lucid Dreams (WILD)

With the powerful and unique technique, Wake-Induced Lucid Dreams, or WILD, you can enter a lucid dream without losing consciousness. This fascinating approach is distinct from other lucid dreaming approaches, which typically include realizing that you are dreaming while already in the dream state.

With WILD, you can watch and actively participate in constructing your dream world by staying awake and aware before you go to sleep. This level of awareness and control can result in vivid and captivating dreams that give you a sense of exploration and adventure.

Though the concept of WILD may sound difficult, many people who have experienced lucid dreams have discovered that it is a natural process that happens when they are very calm or wake up and go back to sleep. Essentially, the WILD method enhances and directs this organic phenomenon to yield a more consistent and manageable encounter.

The main distinction between Finger-Induced Lucid Dreams (FILD) and Mnemonic-Induced Lucid Dreams (MILD) is the level of conscious awareness at the moment of the dream state transformation. Unlike FILD and MILD, which require entering the dream state initially and then lucidly accessing it by identifying mnemonic devices or dream signals, WILD entails maintaining an unbroken stream of consciousness as you enter the dream realm.

Although the Wake-Induced Lucid Dreams (WILD) technique can be challenging, you can develop the skills necessary to access this unique state of consciousness with practice and the procedures mentioned below. Remember that patience and practice are crucial because everyone's experience with WILD differs.

Decide on the right time: The optimal time to try WILD is during rapid eye movement (REM) sleep cycles when dreams are most likely to occur. A common strategy successful lucid dreamers use is setting an alarm for four or six hours of sleep and then trying WILD as they go back to sleep.

Relax your body: Before you begin, ensure you are in a comfortable posture and lying on your side. Close your eyes and focus on progressively relaxing. With this, you can achieve the deep physical relaxation needed for WILD.

Remain mentally alert: Keeping your mind clear is important even when your body relaxes. One helpful method is to employ a mental anchor, such as counting breaths or repeating a mantra. This will help prevent your thoughts from drifting off to sleep and your body from unwinding.

Be mindful of hypnagogic imagery: The patterns, colours, and shapes behind your closed eyelids can become more noticeable as you approach the boundary between wakefulness and sleep. When you see these images, try not to become overly attached to them. This will help you remain objective and in charge.

Enter a dream state. As the hypnagogic imagery grows more vivid and surreal, you will observe a shift in perspective. This is the point where you are going to enter the dream state. Imagine yourself going into a dream sequence or accomplishing a goal, like opening a door or climbing a ladder, to aid you in this process. You can anchor your awareness in the dream domain by actively viewing this.

When fully immersed in the dream, perform a reality check to confirm your lucidity. This may be staring at a digital clock, jumping to see if you can float. If the reality check is successful, then this is a lucid dream.

Explore and enjoy: Now that you've gained clarity, you can go further into your dream world, alter the environment, and engage with dream characters. Remember that remaining awake and in charge is crucial to extending the length of your lucid dream experience.

Gaining Mastery Over Lucid Dream

Believe in your abilities.

Have faith in your ability to fly if, in a dream, you're perched on a precipice. You will tumble into your imagined self even if you know you're dreaming and should be flying. If, in the remote chance, you expect to feel pain after the fall, you will.

If you believe in anything, everything you imagine in your dreams will pass. When you have faith in your ability to do a task, self-assurance is essential, and Lucid will release fear and relinquish control over the unfathomable situation you have imagined.

Start a magical diary.

The secret to becoming Lucid is having a firm grasp of your imagination and dream memories. Keeping a fantasy notebook helps you achieve both of these objectives. A fantasy notebook could be as straightforward as a winding mechanism-equipped scratchpad or intricately customised as a calfskin-bound diary. Either way, the presence of the equivalent is justified. Every night, you should have a pen and journal close to your bed. As soon as you wake up, go over your dreams. Jot down any memories you may have of your dreams as quickly as you can. A comprehensive description ought to be provided! Every morning, review your diary entries and consider all of your fantasies. As you log more of your nocturnal activities, you'll find that you often dream about almost the same subjects. Anything, such as your sister, pet, the sea, school, snakes, etc, could be recurring in your dreams. Dream signals are these recurrent components of dreams; they are a creative first step towards lucid dreams. Some persons, locations, events, and situations recur in dreams repeatedly—something you may not even be aware of now. It's a great approach to reach clarity to use those particular dream signs as tourist sites in the fantasy world once you can recognise them.

Create uncomfortable wake-up calls during the day.

Material science will usually go fuzzily in dreams, except lucid dreams. We can tell when we are dreaming when we have a rude awakening. Use little, painful awakenings to start this process in your conscious existence. Turn on and off the lights several times when you enter a room. As you practise this, consciously focus on your actions and admit that you know your environment. When you eventually become Lucid in your dreams, you can simply acknowledge this to yourself by identifying two or three unpleasant awakenings that are common for you.

My all-time favourite forcefully awakens it, making it aware that gravity is my anchor and forcing it to stare at my feet. I almost feel myself getting ready to float a few crawls above the floor while having a Lucid dream. Acquire Lucid around dusk by forcing him to wake up ten times daily.

Asking yourself, "Am I dreaming?" daily can help you train your mind to ask the same question when you're in a fantasy.

As it is, the trick includes pausing and thinking about it so you can usually tell if you're dreaming or not. Your sense of insanity will be confirmed when you have your first vivid dream, even if it may seem absurd to pose this question when you are certain that you are conscious. Before long, you'll pretend to have a rude awakening and realise, "Wait a minute, it worked! I'm dreaming right now.

Consider it twice a day, at the very least.

Having a clean mind when you sleep is essential, particularly if trying to achieve lucid dreaming, because introspection generally encourages an optimistic mindset. Since mental health influences many aspects of life, including dreaming, everyone should aim for it.

Give it some thought once during the day, at any convenient time, and once again thirty minutes before going to bed. When using this contemplative technique, you should have enough time to arrange your thoughts and prepare before starting your lucid dreaming exercises. Take dietary supplements designed to help induce lucid dreams.

Dream-enhancing enhancements can improve the quality of profound sleep, or Rapid Eye Movement (REM) sleep, even though they do not affect your prosperity. Dreams are supposed to materialise during that particular stage of sleep. The more advantageous you are overall, the more your imagining cycles are more valuable.

Start with a daily multivitamin and supplement with extra fish oil, choline, and magnesium—all known to enhance brain health. Melatonin is also a practical and efficient sedative. As always, if you have any medical conditions or are already taking any drugs, consult your primary care provider before beginning any new improvements.

The last thing you should do before going to bed is meditate, either silently or in secret. Say something like, "I will dream today around evening time, and I will know that I am dreaming," repeatedly until you fall asleep. Recall to visualise your memory aid state as the previously described one. The more you can identify with your practice, the more incredible it will be.

Don't give up if you don't get a Lucid dream as soon as you'd like. Following these suggestions will increase your chances of lucid dreams, but it's not guaranteed. Like anything in life, the more work and attention you put into this, the higher the probability that you will dream yourself into Lucidity.

DREAM MANAGEMENT: STRATEGIES AND METHODS

Have you ever thought of being in charge of your dream? Are you curious about your chances of being successful in doing so?

People have been utilising lucid dreaming techniques to control their dreams since ancient times. Though this can be terrifying initially, in this chapter, we will explore how to produce lucid dreams and address any fear that may accompany them.

You'll acquire the skill and confidence you need in no time at all to bravely venture into your fantasy realm! We'll also go over several techniques for triggering lucid dreams and how to stay in control during them. By the time you finish this chapter, you'll be ready to overcome any challenge your goals may present!

Dream Handling

Purposefully manipulating a dream involves altering the scenarios, people, and settings that arise within the dream. Lucid dreaming is a powerful method for controlling your dreams and unleashing your inner creativity. It's waking up while still asleep, allowing you to take charge of your dream and mould it into what you want.

People have been attracted to the possibility of having lucid dreams for many years, which has led to the development of many strategies for controlling dreams. These strategies include visualising the outcome you want, repeating affirmations or mantras, meditating or using relaxation techniques, and performing reality checks, which involve asking oneself whether something is indeed happening. Through these techniques, practitioners will eventually be able to recognise when they are dreaming and wake up.

It can be difficult or frightening to venture into lucid dreaming for the first time. However, with good instruction and practice, you can easily get used to going into a dream state and maintain control throughout. If you are in a scary dream, try centring yourself with affirmations like "I am safe" or "I have complete control here." In addition, integrate peaceful practices such as deep breathing exercises or visualisation techniques akin to meditation into your dream state to attain increased serenity.

I can still clearly recall my first lucid dream. I was strolling down a dim alleyway when, all of a sudden, I saw something was off. The objects were floating midair like balloons, and the sky was pinkish-purple instead of blue. Then it dawned on me, "Ah!" This can just be a dream. That realisation gave me a tremendous sensation of power and freedom, so I decided to take charge of the situation by altering the landscape. In a matter of minutes, I was flying far above towns and oceans, feeling incredibly satisfied and free!

Since that encounter many years ago, I have continued experimenting with many approaches to lucid dreaming, ranging from strategies to induce Lucidity (such as mnemonic induction) to useful advice on maintaining attention in the dream state (such as counting fingers). Simply put, lucid dreaming gives us access to our inner selves and expands our horizons by using our ideas and thoughts!

Fears Linked to Hallucinogenic Dreams

When experimenting with lucid dreaming, it's typical to have anxiety. It makes sense, after all, to have a small amount of anxiety while dealing with the unknown.

People often worry that they won't be able to regulate their lucid dreams because they think they will become too intense or chaotic. If you have the right tools and techniques, you can become an expert at controlling your lucid dreaming experience to the fullest extent possible. It might be scary to explore parts of oneself you are not familiar with because you might see shadows and feel afraid of not knowing. Maintaining lucid dreams for a long time could be challenging because of these things. Still, you will completely control your active imagination if you are prepared and in the right mindset.

The worry of making mistakes in a lucid dream, which could have real-world consequences, can give rise to feelings of shame and anxiety. People frequently experience anxiety when faced with the possibility of doing something that could have unintended consequences and cannot undo any potential harm.

A third prevalent apprehension around lucid dreaming is that, if not conducted appropriately and under appropriate supervision, it may result in psychological addiction, sleep paralysis, or even nightmares, among other mental health problems. Many people are afraid to try because they don't know enough about lucid dreaming and are concerned about potential negative effects.

When first beginning a lucid dreaming adventure, these worries are normal but may be conquered with practice and patience. Keep alert and mindful to maximise your dream state and maintain control. If you start to feel anxious, take a few deep breaths or repeat encouraging statements to regain equilibrium.

Fortunately, there are ways to get over these anxieties.

Recognising the source of your fear is the first step. Do you fear that you won't be able to control the dream? Or that a horrible thing might occur? You can deal with such problems after determining what is causing your dread. For instance, you can employ visualisation exercises to help you stay grounded and focused during dreams if you are afraid of losing control of them.

Talking about your dreams with a trustworthy friend who will listen to you and encourage you without passing judgment can help reduce your anxiety about lucid dreaming. This can be a useful tactic to alleviate some of those concerns and obtain a deeper comprehension from the viewpoint of another.

Remember that lucid dreaming is a fantastic tool for personal development. Countless creative potential exist when you learn to take charge of your dreams and explore the unknown depths of this universe! Thus, do not allow fear to stand in your quest to become aware of anything special. Making progress towards being an expert in lucid dreaming will take time if you are committed, diligent, and have faith in yourself.

Ways To Interpret Dreams

It is well known that dream interpretation has been used as a therapeutic tool for a very long time. When done correctly, dream analysis can help one become more self-aware by exploring their subconscious and emotional state. By examining numerous methods for dream analysis and interpretation, this chapter invites you to broaden your toolkit of interpretation skills and gain insight into the complex and varied world of dream symbolism. It covers several dream analysis methodologies, including Jungian dream analysis, cognitive dream interpretation, Freud's psychoanalytic method, and journaling and visualization as methods for intuitive reflection.

Interpretation of Jungian Dreams

Jungian dream analysis includes the study of individual and social subconscious themes, archetypal symbols, and dream interpretation techniques. It is based on the idea that dreams facilitate communication between your conscious and subconscious minds. This approach introduces anima/animus, shadow, and the individuation process. Jung created these archetypes based on his research into the relationship between symbols and the human mind. The concept of the ego, an entity made up of conscious concepts and consciousness, was developed by the father of psychoanalysis, Carl Jung. But these concepts are nothing compared to what's hidden in the subconscious, which is why dream analysis is helpful.

The shadow is the darkest side of your psyche. It's also the easiest to obtain and most approachable in a dream. In dreams, your shadow can take the form of someone else, usually of the same gender, or it can appear as symbols or dark, forbidden dream experiences. The anima represents the feminine urges and characteristics seen in men's psyches. Similarly, the animus personifies characteristics and tendencies associated with men and appears in women's subconscious. These two are even more hidden than the shadow and are rarely encountered in the real world, but they may appear in dreams. When dealing with the hate, they take on the persona of a rational being; when dealing with the anima, they adopt the persona of a compassionate being. Dream encounters with the animus, anima, or shadow elicit emotions and thoughts you would never have thought possible in the outside world. This results in a deep realization of who you are (the total of your conscious and subconscious experiences), enabling you to use dreams to reveal hidden facets of your identity and get closer to self-realization.

The following is how to use Jungian dream analysis:

To help you remember your dreams, locate a quiet place where you won't be disturbed.

Recall your dreams and start analyzing them once your body and mind are at rest. Keep an open mind when deciphering your dream encounters.

Since dreams are not meant to be strictly understood, you need to relate your experiences to internal experiences—

that is, what your conscious mind is aware of. Any emotion you experience or whatever your senses identify as being inside your body could be included in this.

Think about each of the different dream elements. You can write them down to help you analyze them more quickly. Once you've noted them, consider what seems to be the purpose behind them. Consider the possible messages that your dreams' symbols, feelings, or visuals might be trying to convey to you. Analyze them from a variety of perspectives to comprehend their importance more fully.

Observe any recurring patterns or symbols. To achieve this, you might need to look at several future dreams to see whether they are similar. Some of the symbols or patterns may have special significance for you. Examine them closely to make sure you don't miss anything.

After identifying recurrent symbols or patterns in your dreams, consider their possible meanings. Are they trying to say anything in particular to you? Additionally, you might think about posing any of the following queries to yourself while you analyze your dream:

What was your initial feeling upon awakening from a dream?

What else did you see in your dream besides the details that caught your attention?

Did you hear a specific sound, song, or voice in your dream?

In your dream, did you observe any humans or animals?

What happened when you were dreaming?

What feelings did you have in your dream?

Give yourself time to reflect on your answers to these questions and what you learned. It's a good idea to jot down any insights you may have, including thoughts and feelings regarding your dream experiences, in your notebook after answering the questions. Small graphics can also be used to highlight a particularly thought-provoking passage.

Some dream interpretations will surprise you because the subconscious doesn't provide signals that the conscious mind is aware of. Several factors need to be considered to determine the dream interpretation. For example, intelligent interpretation is neither self-congratulatory nor self-inflating because you will seldom get information that is wholly positive and free of any negativity. Similarly, if you interpret your dream as a way to blame others for your misfortune, you are generally misinterpreting it. The only one who can learn from your dream encounters is you. Any other person that appears in your dreams is a mirror image of you.

Alternatively, you may tell them about your dreams. You may gain an even deeper understanding if you tell a friend, family member, or therapist about your dream experiences.

The Jungian dream interpretation method suggests that you can learn by making your dreams more symbolic. To do this, you must delve deeper into the significance of the scene, encounter, or symbol that most stuck out in your dream. Consider each symbol's cultural meanings, archetypal importance, and personal relevance when doing this.

Dream Structure

If you've ever watched the British classic Doctor Who, you may be familiar with the words "wibbly-wobbly, timey-wimey stuff". In a very eloquent approach, the Doctor explains why time is non-linear and nonsensical. Dreams function in the same way. You may find that, despite your immediate impression, your dream is somewhat confusing when you reflect on it or record it in writing. It may have featured strangers, started in the middle of a story and then picked up where it left off or involved random, unrelated happenings. If we could somehow link our brains to a TV, we could see how incredibly strange our dreams are.

This may depend in part on how long you spend in each stage of sleep. Other factors include how many hours you sleep each night, how long you sleep, and how often you wake up during the night. Your dreams are determined by your sleep-wake cycles. However, you can train yourself to dream more frequently, resulting in dreamlike experiences. But first, take some time to study and understand how dreams are put together.

Stages of Sleep

You will read about the different sleep stages in the following sections. Scientists divide these several stages into "REM sleep" and "Non-REM sleep." You will see that the bright phase is short, and the deep phase is probably shorter than expected. Remember that although there are only three sleep phases, you will experience each multiple times while in slumber. You won't feel comfortable waking up until you've completed several phases.

Aware Phase

You are not sleeping, even though you appear to be awake. The time you spend awake and sleeping in bed is all that is included in the waking phase. Most people take their time falling asleep, and many of us use our phones in bed. The wake phases (before and after sleep) specify these times. In addition, the majority of people wake up in the middle of the night for a variety of reasons, such as having to go to the bathroom, having a bad dream, or being startled by an unexpected external stimulus (like a bright light, a loud noise, or a little child informing you that they're sick).

Lowering the amount of distractions during the wake phase is advantageous.

For now, just keep in mind that you will find it simpler to get into the light sleep phase if there is less light and noise during the before-sleep wake period. In chapter four, you will learn more about creating a conducive sleep environment.

Light Sleep

Light sleep, the initial sleep phase, usually heralds the transition to deeper sleep. You could wake up fast even when you had just gone to sleep. Specifically, light sleep happens when you nap. There are two parts to the light stage sleep. There is a maximum ten-minute duration to this first stage. Your muscles will start physically relaxing, your breathing and pulse rate will slow, and your body temperature will drop.

In the second light sleep stage, brain waves occur more often. This stage could take anywhere from thirty to sixty minutes to complete. If you plan to take a quick nap, try to wake up toward the end of this period. If not, you'll be drained and agitated when you wake up.

Prolonged Silence

It is exceedingly difficult for someone to wake you in a deep sleep. It is the most reparative stage, allowing your body to repair any damage. If you have ever fallen asleep with a headache and woken up feeling better, you have experienced deep sleep. It's remarkable that deep sleep only lasts for twenty to forty minutes.

In terms of your body, a restful night's sleep lowers blood pressure, increases blood flow to your muscles, and releases hormones that support self-healing. These hormones will promote tissue development and cell repair. Your brain is also getting rid of junk. Getting up from deep sleep is challenging, and when you do, you'll feel disoriented and disoriented. You become less sensitive to outside stimuli while you sleep deeply.

REM sleep

This is going to become exciting. Your mind is most likely to recover. At this point, your brain can solve intricate puzzles, enhance memory, and, yes, even dream. While in REM sleep, your brain encodes the memories from the previous day into your long-term memory. It's a vital and immensely fascinating period of sleep.

Your respiration and heart rate will quicken, your body won't be able to regulate its temperature, and your mental activity will be quite high. It's fascinating to observe that to keep you from living out your dreams, your body will immobilize. A rise in blood flow to the genitalia also accounts for the phenomenon known as "wet dreams," which many teenagers encounter. Anyone may also find that they are dreaming indecently about their workplace. The sudden jerking of your eyes in all directions is called fast eye movement (here's a fun fact you can learn for free).

You should expect to enter REM sleep roughly ninety minutes after falling asleep and stay there for an hour or more. Your body will go through each stage of non-REM sleep before entering the REM stage.

FAQ Regarding Dreams

People spend their entire lives studying the ins and outs of dreams, which makes sense, given how fascinating the subject is. For those of us without the luxury of time, having a concise handbook that addresses some of the most frequently asked questions regarding dreams can be useful. They certainly don't answer all of your questions about dreams, but they could be a great place to start.

Number of Dreams

By now, you should be familiar with every stage of sleep, including the fact that. You also know that you will cycle through each phase several times while you sleep. Then, how often will you dream at night? You may think you only dream once or twice because you don't remember most of them. Studies show that most people forget 95% of their dreams (Cherry, 2019). You will probably dream four or six times in a typical night. Some have even reported having as many as twelve dreams in one night. The difference in duration between these dreams can be explained by the fact that your REM stages get longer as you go through each phase. Still, most academics agree that most people dream for about two hours every night. But worry not—sleeping soundly is not hampered by dreams. Dreams are perfectly normal and healthy during the night.

Ways To Get Lucid Dreams

Science has shown that lucid dreaming is real, and anyone can experience it, no matter who they are. Trial by trial is carried out in labs by experts in sleep or dreams. Techniques for helping people realize lucid dreaming were created due to the experiments.

However, laboratories do not produce lucid dreaming. It has been practised by monks, mystics, yogis, shamans, sufis, and spiritualists worldwide since ancient times. The techniques were with them. Nonetheless, modern terminology and methods are developed by laboratories and are, in certain aspects, quicker and simpler. Many thanks to the experts in the lab.

Mnemonics-Induced Lucid Dreams (MILD)

Dr. Stephen LaBerge created this technique while he was getting his PhD. This approach consists of four steps. The secret to utilizing this method is creating or initiating your present dream by remembering your past. Let's investigate this.

Making Notes and Keeping the Dream in Mind

During this phase, keep a dream journal beside your head pillow. Every time you wake up from a slumber, jot down what you recall from the dream. You're not an artist, but write down the time and date and, if necessary, sketch down everything you remember from the dream.

Not every dream can be remembered. Most dreams are too hazy to remember, even the biggest pictures we could have seen. If you can't remember ever having a dream, it's possible that you never had one.

To find out if your notes relate to your current emotional, physical, or environmental state, you can go over them in advance. For example, you may find a link between what happened to you and what happened in your dream. Alternatively, you can observe what happens in the days that come after your dream and think that this is how it is happening. It seems unrelated to lucid dreaming, but it can help persuade your subconscious that a dream will occur whenever you experience a significant event.

Verifications of Reality

Exercises called "reality checks" might increase your awareness of the distinctions between dreams and reality. Naturally, we usually notice the distinctions. This isn't usually how dreams operate, though. We cannot tell the difference between reality and the dream since everything in the dream exists outside of our conscious awareness.

Dreams are windows into the actual world. Verify that when you dream, it is truly a dream. That's the primary notion. You must get into the habit of checking in with reality to facilitate this process when you dream. If you don't develop the habit, you won't do it in the dream.

According to lucid dreamers, you should press your palm or finger firmly against the wall, aiming for the finger to pass through the wall without breaking. It can happen in a dream but won't happen in the real world. As your awareness of reality increases, so will your consciousness of the dream.

If acting on dreams becomes second nature to you, you'll behave in a semi-automatic way. If you know you are dreaming, you have succeeded in entering lucid dreaming. Of course, there are other ways to verify reality, including using arithmetic problems, mirror reflections, or burning your fingertip, although I wouldn't suggest it.

Absurd Confirmations

Make false impressions to your subconscious that you are dreaming when you are not. You may have random visions, both physically and emotionally, as you relax this evening. Every time this happens, remind yourself that "I am dreaming" or "the next vision will be a dream."

If you consistently carry out your purposeful activities, your subconscious mind will start to execute them as if they were commands. Assume for a moment that you are ready to retire to bed. You will dream into the next scene or vision if your subconscious follows your commands. However, that is not the end of this tactic. It is said that if you are in the so-called hypnagogic state marked by vivid images, you can follow the fourth stage to obtain the perfect lucid dream.

Dream Analysis

Sometimes, beginners miss this stage because they fall asleep so quickly. It is unrelated to this to dream while you are awake. This is completed when you are about to go to sleep and wake up. You do this when your mind and body are relaxed, and your vivid random pictures occur: to use the language of the "human" race. These two conditions need to be satisfied.

To imagine a dream, you have to immerse yourself in it. When you visualize, don't limit your perspective. Remember to include the other sensors as well. For example, a simple location representation is not a good visualization. The best strategy is to place yourself in that circumstance.

After you get "there," the only thing left to lucid dreaming is that awareness that you are dreaming.

How is MILD run?

Perhaps you've seen that those procedures don't directly relate to one another. It appears that lucid dreaming can be attained in just one or two steps.

But in reality, it's not. It operates in this manner.

Dreams are experiences that you can remember. However, to recall the dream, we must be able to recall it. Dream memory is a sign that dreams are real. But unless they are vivid, dreams are hard to remember. To remember dreams, we must record them using a particular technique. If you don't write down the dream as soon as you wake up, it will gradually slip your mind. If you engage in other activities before writing it, your brain triggers the cell to become active. After that, your dream recollection gradually disappears.

We must be able to recall the dream's appearance, sounds, sensations, and other specifics. We perform reality checks to assist us in differentiating between the dream and the real world. Lucid dreaming is triggered by a sensation we get when dreaming, which is different from reality.

You try to remember the dream before you go to sleep now that you are aware of and experiencing it. However, there are instances when your subconscious mind keeps you from experiencing it. Your brain operates according to hard-to-change rules. Its defence is on the edge of your conscious mind, midway between your waking and sleep cycles. Affirmation has a similar purpose to command. Repeat that the affirmation is the same as you add the command to the queue. When you go to sleep, your subconscious mind will execute that directive first.

You must provide cues to help your subconscious mind know where to send you when it executes this command. That's the place and time your dream imagery is active. If you forget this step, your unconscious mind will take you back to the dream you either dreamed or remembered. But instead of experiencing the clear dream you want, you'll lapse into a mediocre dream that's not as vivid.

These steps enable you to run an integrated process. They are related to one another. Lucid dreaming can be intentionally induced by following the phases. But it doesn't always work in a single night. Give it a little time. If lucid dreaming was as easy as having a typical dream, Dr. Stephen LaBerge would never have been awarded his PhD.

In Real Life Versus In Dreams

What were your thoughts on these activities like lucid dreaming? Your dream existence benefits greatly from what you have just learned in the real world. Dreamworlds are rich in multimodal experiences: hearing, feeling, thinking, tasting, and seeing. The main difference between the real world and the dream world is the source of the experience. The real world exposes you to external stimuli, but the experience of the dream world originates from within. Because all of these sensations can be so disorienting, many people question whether they are awake or just dreaming. You can tell your mental state because your conscious mind helps you choose between truth and imagination. Dreams tend to narrow your senses by making you aware of only what is directly in front of you; in reality, however, awareness can be expanded to include things like hearing sounds on the street or outside your current place.

Since the actions and visuals in your dreams are not real, you will often be able to identify when you are dreaming. For example, you might not even live close to the ocean or be at the beach and not remember how to get there. Another example would be changes in the properties of your body; you would feel a distorted shape or be able to press your fingers through it. Another example would be looking about you in your dream for strange animals, landscapes, or anything that doesn't seem realistic. You will become aware that you are dreaming and not in reality because your conscious mind is active during a dream.

Sometimes, it's difficult to distinguish between dreams and reality when someone experiences a false awakening. False awakenings occur when you wake up from a dream only to discover that you are still asleep or "trapped" in a dream state. You come to realize this a few moments later. Many people find this disturbing and worry that they are stuck in their dreams and won't be able to escape. Finding out later that your fantasy of waking up, taking a shower, and beginning your day is not true is one of the most upsetting false awakenings. Reality checking is essential in this case since it uses your conscious awareness to ascertain if you are awake or dreaming.

Benefits of Illusionary Dreams

By now, you should be more familiar with the details of lucid dreaming. I get excited at lucid dreaming because it's such an incredible experience! There are several reasons why lucid dreaming might be beneficial. Even if it doesn't seem conceivable, everything is within your reach when you dream about it.

reduces Mental Pain

Lucid dreaming is a means of escaping reality. It's an excellent way to escape melancholy, anxiety, or depression. Many persons with insomnia, or the inability to fall or stay asleep at night, discover that experiencing lucid dreams improves their sleep quality by providing them with something to look forward to.

Reduce Nightmares and Overcome Fears
Everyone has certain fears, and some people even have nightmares. Sometimes, when nightmares about your worries take over your sleep, you could find yourself tossing and turning in bed. Lucid dreaming is terrifying, but it may also be an escape route and coping mechanism. Make use of lucid

dreams as a secure space to work through nightmares and overcome anxiety. You control your dreams, so promote lucid dreaming to prevent nightmares. If you have lucid nightmares, you can change the course of your dreams.

One typical way to address their fear is to use lucid dreaming. You have the power to create fear and deal with it safely since you are in control of the dream world, or you can decide to stop it altogether. For example, if you have arachnophobia, which is the dread of spiders, you might be able to see yourself approaching a small spider or looking at several ones. The next level could involve visualizing yourself holding a dangerous spider in your palm. You can wake up from the dream and return to safety at any time. You'll eventually get used to seeing spiders in real life and learn not to run out of the room at the first hint of one. Lucid dreaming opens the door to living a brave life and more adventures.

An Alternative Perspective

In lucid dreams, you can think about things you might not normally do. When you're having lucid dreams, your mind and soul start talking to you; many people find they're talking to themselves. They ponder the great issues of life, such as what their true purpose is in the present and the future. Suppressed thoughts could surface during lucid dreaming, allowing you to discover more about yourself. You learn more about yourself in a safe space where you are not open to outside criticism.

Dream Company

The best part is that you can have anything you want in your lucid dream since you can set up the dream's storyline before falling asleep. Do you want to see Atlantis by submarine? Yes, without a doubt! What about jumping off the Grand Canyon or saving the world from a supervillain? You are also capable of accomplishing that!

By considering the storyline of your dream and using the wake-induced or dream-induced techniques you will discover later, you can create complex dreams to your heart's content. Create as much anticipation as possible and think about the dream you want to have frequently since lucid dreaming will likely occur when you are excited about a dream.

New Methods and Dimensions for Transportation

You do not need to walk, drive, or use any other typical form of transportation in your lucid dreams. You have a choice in how you want to go! During lucid dreams, people often fly (alone) or spin around to go anywhere they want to be. You can travel to fictional places, different countries, different time zones, and even alternative universes. Try travelling to the past or the future in your lucid dreams; you are working within the constraints of your chosen timeline and need not conform to any real-world qualities.

Overview of Reality Checking

Greetings from Chapter 4 of our lucid dreaming adventure! This chapter will examine reality-checking in detail, a key method that facilitates lucid dreaming. If you've ever wondered how to distinguish between the real world and your dreams, or if you've always wanted to learn the key to conscious control within your dreams, then reality testing is a crucial skill you must learn.

Philosophers, physicists, and intellectuals have been fascinated with the concept of reality for ages. Since Descartes famously stated, "Cogito, ergo sum" (I think, therefore I am), humanity has grappled with the nature of reality and its misleading qualities. This battle has continued through thought-provoking passages in Plato's Allegory of the Cave. In a nutshell, lucid dreaming is an invitation to enter a realm where the mind is unconstrained by the physical world and leaves the confines of our reality.

So, what exactly is reality testing, and why is it required for lucid dreaming? We might apply the reality testing technique to find out if we are dreaming or awake at the moment. It facilitates the identification and induction of lucid dream states by acting as a bridge between our aware and unconscious thoughts. We develop a regular inclination to question the reality around us and increase our self-awareness by including reality checks in our daily routines.

We rely on our senses throughout our waking hours to provide an accurate picture of the outside world. We rely on the senses of sight, hearing, touch, taste, and smell as indicators of reality. However, the laws of the dream realm are distinct; they often contradict logic and distort our perception. Challenge the principles of physics and challenge the basis of our comprehension. This is the realm that lucid dreaming allows us to consciously enter and navigate, transforming our dreams into colourful, infinite play spaces.

Examining our reality acts as a compass, guiding us through our dreams' labyrinthine corridors. By incorporating specific techniques and routines into our daily lives, we can start to unravel the mysteries of our dreamscapes and develop a keen awareness of the distinctions between reality and the dream state. Through deliberate and systematic reality testing, we hone our ability to recognize the minute cues and contradictions that define the dream state.

In reality testing, several techniques may be applied to differentiate between dreams and reality. Common reality tests include watching your hands, paying attention to how clocks and text messages work, switching light switches, looking in mirrors, and attempting gravity-defying leaps. These checks serve as triggers, promoting dream lucidity and making us reflect on the nature of our current experience.

But reality testing is more than just a collection of steps. It's a mindset penetrating our waking hours—a persistent mix of curiosity and cynicism. It challenges us to face our assumptions, look at the basis of our reality, and live in the now. Fostering this way of thinking makes us deeply used to self-reflection and questioning the accuracy of our experiences and the outside world.

In the following sections, we'll look at the various reality testing techniques and how. We'll also cover how to make reality testing a regular part of your routine so that it becomes instinctive. We'll discuss common issues and possible risks to assist you in overcoming uncertainty and fortifying your link to the dream world.

As we show the substantial impact reality testing can have on your lucid dreaming practice, get ready for an insightful and illuminating journey. By improving your ability to discriminate between dreams and reality, you may take charge of the narrative of your dream experiences and gain more agency within your dreamscape. To fully realize the incredible potential of lucid dreaming, let's embrace the mysteries that lie outside the confines of reality and collaborate to employ reality testing.

Dream Interpretation and Handling

Dreams are common occurrences. Dreams can be frightening, instructive, illuminating, or just plain scary. Many people are curious about how their dreams are interpreted. Some dreams could make you excited, while others might make you afraid. When people wake up from sleep, they feel the same feelings as if their dreams were genuine. Because of this, many people research dream management strategies to help them control their emotions.

So, is it possible to control a dream? According to studies, it's possible to control your dreams, which can be helpful, especially for people sick of nightmares. Now that they have control over the dream, they may transform the horror into a happily ever after. Researchers have discovered that you can control your dreams and use them to heal yourself and decompress.

Dreams are:

Just your rearranged thoughts.

Feelings.

Visual impressions from the day.

Lucid dreaming, on the other hand, is awareness associated with your dream. Metacognition is the understanding and knowledge of your thoughts and is associated with lucid dreaming. A recent study found a strong association between metacognition and lucid dreaming, with those who are more skilled at it having a higher likelihood of experiencing lucid dreams (Pauley, 2017).

Why Would You Want to Be in Charge of Your Dream?

With the help of lucid dreams, you can unlock the subconscious and solve some of life's mysteries. You can eliminate strong or disturbing feelings just by consciously controlling your dream. You can discover who you truly are by analyzing your perfect world. Your subconscious may appear strange initially, but you will become used to it.

People who experience nightmares are deeply dedicated to attaining lucid dreaming and healing this condition. Lucid dreaming might help you put an end to your sorrows and anxieties. You can also see loved ones who have passed away in your dreams. You can hug them and converse with them as though they were in your subconscious. Perhaps you can even feel their warmth, depending on how focused your thoughts are.

How to Govern and Shape Your Dreams

Try These Techniques for Dream Awareness

Write down your dream: Try to write down your dream as soon as you wake up each time to help you remember it better. Stay still for a short while after waking up and try to remember the dream. To have lucid dreams, the dream needs to be recalled.

Examine your situation: A reality check is essential to realizing your dreams. Try examining your hands and feet, glancing around, prodding your skin, and checking the clock, among other reality checks.

To assist yourself in recalling the mnemonic for lucid dreaming, say aloud, "I know that I will be in a dream", before turning in for the evening. You'll be able to tell dreams from reality as a result.

Dream symbols that keep coming back: Grab a journal and go over your dreams to look for any themes or patterns that keep coming up. In dreams, things can recur; all you need to do is recognize these occurrences to be aware of them.

Simply return to your slumber. When you wake up, try to remember your dream as well as you can. At that point, you can go back to sleep. You will usually have lucid dreams after doing this when you completely control your actions.

Chapter 4: The Effects of LSD

Effects often become noticeable 20 minutes after ingestion. When tingling occurs throughout the body, the medication has most likely reached the user's bloodstream. The effects typically reach their zenith an hour after this initial impact. The user's pupils dilate at this stage due to their body temperature rising and their heart rate quickening. There can be a few peak hours when hallucinations first appear. Colours could appear more vibrant and sound richer. Users could see small details that they had never noticed before.

The customer usually feels less energized when the trip eventually wears off. LSD users experience psychological effects that cause them to remember either a good or bad trip. The memories and effects last a lifetime, but they gradually fade in the absence of records.

The effects of LSD range from mild to potent. There could be impacts that are sensory, psychological, or physical. Numerous negative and positive side effects of LSD are known to exist.

A common adverse consequence that many LSD users encounter is known as a "bad trip." A trip that goes wrong is referred to as a bad trip. Trips that go badly are compared to living hell by those who have experienced them.

Impacts on the Human Body

The way the body reacts to LSD can be both general and highly variable. Common physical repercussions include the following:

Reduced Appetite

LSD can promote weight loss because of this effect. Water weight often accounts for the majority of weight loss after using LSD.

Not getting enough sleep.

It may be difficult for someone who frequently experiences hallucinations to go to sleep at night, especially if they are frightening.

Dilation of Students

Pupil contraction is triggered by certain brain receptors, which psychedelics can block, which is why dilated pupils can occur when using them. When the pupils can no longer contract, dilation takes place.

Cottonmouth

A parched mouth characterizes the disease. LSD produces a malfunction in the salivary glands, leading to a dry mouth.

numbness

Users often report experiencing tingling or losing feeling in their fingers and toes during an LSD trip. Often, this sensation is paired with an atypical coldness in the fingers and/or toes.

emesis

It's common to feel sick as the trip approaches its peak, particularly if you're travelling on an empty stomach.

Overheating or Underheating

Both conditions are acknowledged as adverse effects of LSD. However, they are typically linked to LSD overdose.

High Body Core Temperature

It is common for hallucinogen users to have fluctuations in body temperature. This phenomenon is referred to as drug-induced fever or drug-induced hyperthermia.

chills

LSD-induced chills are not uncommon. This phenomenon is known as "acid chills."

Perspiration

Some LSD users tend to sweat a lot when they use the substance. Some people may experience anxiousness in addition to the increased body warmth that comes with travelling.

High Blood Pressure

The fact that LSD raises blood pressure cannot be avoided. When an LSD user takes more of the drug, their blood pressure responds by rising.

Elevated Heart Rate

When using LSD, there may be a minor or noticeable rise in heart rate. Sometimes, having a high heart rate while travelling might make the trip uncomfortable, especially if the user is ill.

Impacts on the Emotions

While reports of LSD's psychological side effects vary, the following are the most frequently mentioned impacts on the mind:

Illusions

The most common adverse consequence of consuming LSD, one of the most potent hallucinogens on the market, is this. A hallucination is a state where the senses are tricked. The primary feature of horrible trips is that while some hallucinations may be beautiful and enjoyable, others may be terrifying. If someone is absorbed in their delusion, they could lose their sense of reality. A less seasoned user, therefore, needs a sober buddy.

Delusions

An individual has a delusion when on LSD, believing ardently in something that is not true, even if it is physically impossible. During a delusional episode, the user's beliefs are unshakeable even when evidence suggests that the views are implausible. You could believe he is the king or aliens have taken over. These delusions may even give rise to paranoia.

A Guide To Lucid Dream Interpretation

Oneironauts, fearless explorers of the dream world, have been looking for a dependable and easy way to induce lucid dreams for a long time. One way to wake up the sleeping brain just enough to induce lucidity without upsetting sleep was to flavour pillows with aromas like lilac, musk, or other perfumes. To drive a lucid dream out of the system, investigators have been regularly awakened in the middle of the night or put under hypnosis. Before turning in for the night, some people have even promised themselves they will have a lucid dream.

But finding a recipe that is guaranteed to bring forth the lucid muse has been more like looking for the Holy Grail than it has been like concocting something in the mind. A person's solution may not work for another. Scholars, however, have not been deterred by this very difficult task, and they have created a variety of reliable, if not comprehensive, induction procedures. These are imperfect maps of a dark planet, some more revealing than others, much like terrestrial mapping. We truly hope this instruction will help you attain the ability to dream clearly. Using a very holistic approach, it compiles the research findings of other authors to familiarize you with the subject matter of this book and help you put all of your goals into perspective.

MENTALE OF PRIMER

Nan-in, a Japanese [Zen] teacher, was approached by a university professor with inquiries concerning Zen. Nan-in was serving tea. He poured till his guest's cup was full. The professor continued to see the overflow until he could take it no more. It's overstuffed. There will be no more admissions! Nan-in replied, "Like this cup, you are full of conjectures and opinions." How can I teach you about Zen if you don't empty your cup first?

Paul Reps., Zen Flesh, Zen Bones

It should not be surprising that regular meditation practice can aid in the induction of lucid dreams if the association between lucid dreaming and meditation is as strong as we think. Studies on meditators' dreams have corroborated the anecdotal evidence that they have a substantially higher incidence of lucid dreams.

Gregory (Scott) Sparrow, the author of the ground-breaking book Lucid Dreaming: Dawning of the Clear Light, was among the first to see the connection between lucid dreaming and meditation. He said, "I soon noticed that lucidity emerged predictably after a deep or fulfilling meditation when it started to arise with increasing regularity." It seemed clear that intensely pious living would coexist with lucid dreams. This association became clearer when I began doing fifteen or twenty minutes of early morning meditation (between two and five in the morning). Time and again, as I drifted back to sleep, dreams that were clear for little periods and with incredible clarity would come to me.

Numerous researchers have meticulously examined the possible relationship between meditation and lucid dreaming since Sparrow's discovery. Henry Reed, a psychologist, was the first to conduct research. He found that transparency was more common when a subject had meditated than when he or she had not. Several research have also found this association. In several research involving transcendental meditation (TM) practitioners, Gackenbach and colleagues at Maharishi International University (MIU) have found that meditators regularly report more lucid dreams than control participants.

During shamanic rites, where drumming and chanting produce a condition similar to meditation, lucid dreams are also more likely. For instance, psychology graduate student FaribaBogzaran discovered that when she chanted or listened to drumbeats to produce a shamanic condition before going to sleep, she had about seventeen lucid dreams every month.

A note of caution about the techniques: Sparrow discovered that although lucid dreams frequently followed his predawn meditation practice for "attunement," he did not have lucid dreams if he meditated to produce them. He says, "My dreams severely chastised me for such confounded motives!" "I am gradually learning how to walk carefully."

Gyaltrul Rinpoche, a Tibetan Buddhist monk, reiterates Sparrow's teaching. Gyaltrul highlights in a discussion on the "Tibetan Yoga of the Dream State" that attempting to become conscious when in a state of sleep requires transpersonal aspirations. The monk describes the goal of meditation as "to benefit all sentient beings in order to bring them temporary and permanent happiness," using Buddhist terminology. Put another way, the goal of meditation should not be selfish but rather self-serving.

Although most research linking meditation to lucidity has utilized TM meditators, it seems likely that what is true for TM will also hold for other meditation modalities. Atonement, atonement, emptying the "cup," and consciousness growth are the three main objectives of any meditation. Everybody uses a different approach and style. Some, for example, give you koans or stories to meditate on; others tell you to focus on your breathing and allow all thoughts to come to you. Numerous publications are available to assist you in getting started. Still, it is no coincidence that all reputable meditation schools emphasize the value of having a master or guide to support your efforts. Sometimes, during meditation, unexpected feelings and emotions arise; a more seasoned practitioner can assist you in understanding them.

Observing Spirit Guides and Other Entities

One benefit of Astral Projection is that you may encounter your spirit guide or guides or other entities. Now, along with some self-defence tips and a potential route to meet your spirit guide, I'll go over some of the good and bad entities you may encounter in this chapter.

Spirit guides are angelic beings who help us through life. Some believe that the spirit guide or guides are pre-selected by the higher self, or self before we are born. They may lead you through daily life toward your higher purpose and may also bestow upon you gifts of wisdom, serenity, peace, or a deeper understanding.

Sometimes, other spirits will resurface to support and share wisdom, and our spirit guides will occasionally lead us through life. They could take on the shape of an object, an animal, or a human. They might even be on a different spiritual path. The mentors or guides may also be going through a spiritual development process. Some may be advanced or aware; they could be ascended masters such as Jesus, Buddhas, angels, or even masters of their field. They might identify as ambiguous, feminine, or masculine. They may be allocated to help others in addition to you or assigned to help you alone. They could be spirits once human beings and now dwelling on the astral plane. Perhaps they will only appear when you're ready to welcome them or when you can see them and use their presence to help you achieve your earthly objectives. Astral projection is a great technique to meet them because they can only live in the astral realm.

Watching our lives from start to finish would be an amazing ability for spirit guides. Depending on how far they are in their ascension, they could be able to use this power.

So, how can a spirit guide help you?

You can receive signals from a spirit guide with instructions. This might appear as tangible items, realizations from your physical waking life, or other mysterious symbols.

Emotions can also be aroused in you by spirit guides. They can interact with you telepathically by sending you feelings or emotions and speaking to you audibly. That's what an astral-dimensional being is capable of. Not constrained by the five senses, your spirit self is the source of these messages. Others assert that the heavenly realm speaks symbolic and intuitive language. The next time you see your spirit guide, keep that in mind.

So, what other creatures exist in the afterlife?

A vast, nearly "ecosystem-like" population of beings living in the astral world exists. They can be amiable, strong, compassionate, helpful, or entertaining. They may also be violent, vampiric, destructive, or just plain repulsive. Their degrees of talent and intelligence differ substantially.

Less intelligent animal-like entities might exist in the lower spectrum of the cosmic "ecosystem." They may all operate in the actual world despite their ethereal origins. Some higher-level entities may also possess this power. Not all astral projectors are damaged, but some are, especially the new ones.

Because they are ignorant of other realms, many celestial beings are startled to see an astral traveller. They resemble real people with their objectives and quirks. You never know who you might run up on the road, even if other people do.

Another possibility is to meet angels or angel-like entities. Angels are the highest order of spiritual beings. It's been stated that intentionally bumping into an angel is very tough, if not impossible. They live at the highest cosmic level and are typically unseen. They can manifest in the material world; however, this is extremely rare and significant. The lights might be flickering. Angels still have another purpose.

It is possible to see departed relatives or ancestors in the afterlife. One or more angels are frequently watching them or enabling their communication from a distance, whether they are guiding you or communicating with you. This is not unusual.

One must have the purest intentions to connect with an entity of this kind. Throughout the day, repeat, pray, or meditate with these intentions, and potential contact may arise; however, it is almost always the entity's duty to make contact.

They can occasionally appear as objects, animals, old people, wise men or women, or as young, sensual, attractive, or sexual beings. There's one thing to remember when you see these or any other cosmic entity. Keep your composure and consideration. Refrain from following your instincts, especially when it comes to sex. In the cosmic dimension, like attracts, therefore being nice will lure other nice entities. You generally attract the vibrations you are giving off.

But there are more creatures in the astral plane. I have mentioned the potential to come across demonic or evil spirits. They can range in level from exceedingly dangerous to as low as destructive animals. What should you do if you encounter one of these entities?

Avoidance and evasion are two of the best tactics for dealing with a malignant monster. Return to your body as soon as you detect any evil. Hopefully, the entity will disappear and locate a new victim. The best tactics when dealing with a powerful bad force are avoidance and evasion. You can attempt to liberate yourself from the entity by shifting your energy to a different frequency or entering the heavenly realm and landing on a different plane.

Turn to face them. An entity that refuses to leave you or is a low-level creature may be subject to your ability to banish or dispel it. You can do this by summoning a spirit weapon, an energy shield or sword being an excellent option. Fill your spiritual weapons with the virtues of courage, love, light, peace, and peace. That way, they'll get stronger. The weapons are an expression of who you are. Thus, you can bolster such traits within yourself and launch a further attack by having faith in yourself. Try to diffuse as quickly as possible. If you don't wait to transform back into your physical form until the creature has been defeated, it may resurface in that form or begin to consume your soul.

Beg them to quit causing you trouble. If the entity's power is too great, you may need to back off and show respect for it. If the entity leaves you alone, you may view it as a victory, even if it may feel like a loss. If the entity is very powerful, contact an ascended being immediately for support. Here, an angel or an ascended master are your best options. That's the best course of action when facing a powerful dark force. Angels are some of the most powerful beings in the astral dimension. They can drive out any creature you might encounter and will always come to your aid when you vibrate at the right frequency.

Recall that, similar to the dream realm, you may suffer from physical or spiritual tiredness when you return to the earthly level after fighting a dark force in the heavenly realm or being possessed by one.

It's crucial to show respect to other beings and send out good vibes into the hereafter. I hope that you will come across more like-minded organizations.

www.ingramcontent.com/pod-product-compliance
Lightning Source LLC
Chambersburg PA
CBHW052134110526
44591CB00012B/1711